W Is ?

by **Dana Catharine**
illustrated by Jackie Snider

Printed in the United States of America

ISBN 0-15-317109-X – Where Is Dolly?

Ordering Options
ISBN 0-15-318571-6 (Package of 5)
ISBN 0-15-316985-0 (Grade 1 Package)

2 3 4 5 6 7 8 9 10 179 02 01 00

Where is  ?

1

I am here.

Where is  ?

3

I am here!

Where is  ?

I am here!

Where is  ?

Here is  !

Teacher/Family Member ....

Where Is  **?**

Set out two sheets of paper. Have your child draw a picture on one sheet to show where Dolly was hiding and on the other to show where he or she has found a missing toy.

 School-Home Connection

Ask your child to read *Where Is*  *?* to you. Ask where your child could hide in your home. Play hide-and-seek.

Word Count: 19

Vocabulary Words: Where
is
here

Phonic Elements: Consonants: /m/*m*, /s/*s*
am
is
Short Vowel: /a/*a*
am

....

TAKE-HOME BOOK
Open Doors
Use with "Where Is Sam?"